The Brittle Shards

Gordon Ellis was born in 1948 of Scottish-Irish descent and was brought up between inner city Birmingham and Gourock on the Firth of Clyde, his family having roots in Ballymena in Co.Antrim. He studied philosophy, literature and religion at university and went on to do research in Hindu iconography. He has taught at university in England, practiced as a psychotherapist, and been spiritual director of a Tibetan Buddhist Centre in Cheshire. Poets he has been influenced by include: Ezra Pound, Basil Bunting, W.S.Graham, Ernst Meister, Gunnar Ekelof and Chinese poets of the Tang Dynasty. As well as a number of books of poetry, he has also published several books of essays, including, 'Avoiding Extinction' co-authored with Alexander Matthews. He now lives in South Devon.

Works by Gordon Ellis

Prose

Crossing The Ocean of Existence 2003
Cycling Round Existence (Discovering Aspects of the
Psychopathology of Western Civilisation) 2014
Gordian Knots: Essays 2010-2020
Avoiding Extinction (with Alexander Matthews) 2021

Poetry

Elysian Wiles
The Broken Shards
At Times End
Shades of Non-Existence, Sculptures of the Void

The Brittle Shards

Poems 2010 - 2020

Gordon Ellis

Rootless Tree
www.elysianwiles.com

ISBN: 978-1-9196313-2-5

Contents

The Brittle Shards

Little acts of kindness that have been
Lost in the tumult of distraction.
Little acts of tenderness that have been
Lost in the tumult of distraction.
And between the two an unspeakable world, a void.

Have you seen the trees bathed in golden light?
Many days, many, many days pursued by questions,
Straying like dogs yapping at ankles.
Maintain your demeanour, look away.
Tomorrow there'll be nothing more to say.

Humour me. Count the ripples. Why cast the stone there?
And will you recover it, one day, at the ocean's edge?
Meanwhile, across the street, the shop's window is empty.
Which will come first?
The shutter moves, then the eye closes.

The letter unfolds, encloses space, and dies.
It lies, there on the page, inert and defiant.
But none of this matters; it is all too late.

Is there anything you want to offer me,
Apart from what I have taken?
I have renounced all inheritance:
The wild sparrows, the tame hawk,
The knot of hair you singed with scorn,
The smile preserved in sugar and lies,
A shoe containing shrivelled toes.
Is there something else you have to say,
Something I missed in momentary distraction?

The letters form into strange shapes
As if they have a life of their own.
Is it Sinhalese? No, they are continuing
To unfold. Is it Greek, Arabic? No.
The lines are continuously redrawing
Themselves, and what might have been meant changes.
If only I had that fluidity of movement in space,
There would be no one here to be pinned down,
And I could live my life in any language.

The desert wind, like voile,
Shifting, shadowy like light
Over aeons of desolation,
Missed opportunities,
Car dumps of abandoned dreams,
Meets the solidity of man's ways
And dies, reabsorbed into space.

Don't turn around, the dead may disappear.
You can't entice them into any future.
Custodians of all that's past, let them stay
Hauntingly present in all you do.

Sounds emerge from silence like bodies from the sea,
Dancing upon water, as you count distractedly.
Indeed, every moment counts, and is accounted for,
Like shells that form a noose on which you pull.

Your lips move, your face contorts. I cannot hear
What you say. The air is jagged, frayed.
I am a mask. I'm not how I appear.
The moon is full, however, the rabbit's gone elsewhere.

I dally – my coquette! There's nothing left to screw.
A cello wends its lonely way down passages
Too dark to ascertain; wry nerves, still grins.
My body wracked by long-forgotten pain, resists.
I open my eyes and dream: there is nothing here.
Objects dissolve into space – old sofas, old beds,
Technological wizardry, are reabsorbed
Like icons into cyberspace.

I wait for things to connect.
Nothing happens.
Then you smile.
Standing there holding a small bunch of tulips,
Merged with the sky, naked
And I smile too – what else could I do?

You turned and walked away. I saw you, distant
Dissolving into night, shadow in darkness.
A world I'd never known, although so close,
Another universe of discourse, same words,
Different meanings: the difference of twins
Who expected more, and couldn't settle for less.

The eye of wisdom is shut,
Each follows their own dream.
Each day I become more lost,
And my convictions stronger.
In this babel of voices I trust.
Find the inner voice, I am told.
Flowers bloom in the barren soil,
Apparition of lost souls – listen!

Like The Face of a Cow on the Wall of the Sky

Un monde tres ancient tournoyait dans nos tetes et l'on attendait le moment ou tou allait tomber.

(Pierre Reverdy   'L'Intgrus')

I remove my clothes one by one
Jacket shirt trousers socks underwear
I am not yet naked much is still concealed
Concealing
I remove my hair my skin sinews
Arteries liver kidneys spleen heart lungs
My brain and all my bodily organs
I dismantle my skeleton scatter the bones
Still I am not yet naked much is concealed
Concealing
I discard my thoughts the moods the feelings
That arise in my mind
I dismantle my mind and let it go
There is only the space between objects
No one is there - naked, and dancing apart.

Pallor creeps across your face
Shadows of a lengthening sun
Your eyes blank and watery
Reflect the metal grey of sky
Around your feet twigs dry leaves
And memories to consume you
The prospect of a sedentary life
Slow-burn heart-warming acute
There'll be more for you to do
But nothing grave graveur
A chink of light that etches
On your heart a name
But you will not forget the silence
From which it grows and then returns

Hoopoe on a fence
O bulbul bulbul
Fire consumes
Before rain expires

It is your signature
A clear mark
That blossoms
A seed of life
Before you know it
And you have grown
Flashing myriad smiles
Before a new star
Appears in this constellation

There is no beauty without
The pain that nurtures it
Without the mud - no lotus
And bereft the flower dies

More die in bed than anywhere else
While standing can extend your life
Ergo: don't be a fool sleep standing
O Life *de rigueur* so simple so sublime

I open my skin and step out
I am raw don't touch me
Your tenderness is a searing pain
Your harshness salt that refreshes
People stare to see such splendour
I am radiant with a light that blinds

I am dead no one can hear what I say
I speak like a fish
You blend into the snow
Merge into the mist
There is beauty in this spaciousness
Labile syllables resonate
And manifest as fertile fields
Where crops are harvested
By warriors of truth....
Before dissolving into the wine of life

Behind the mask there is another mask
And behind that mask a third
And so on in a regress that is infinite
The Carnevale - choose your character
Dress your part learn to walk that way
A myriad distinctions fantasies of falsity
This is not your imagination
But your imaginings seem so real
Removed one by one everything is gone
No one can enter the space
That reveals you not even you
I watch the sun setting sky striated
With pink with purple and with grey
The sky is silent now
You are enveloped by that loneliness
You have longed for and dread
You lower your eyes one last time
That is all you know
While others claim much much more:
There is nothing to part from nothing to join.
 'Let go of my balls you are breaking them!'
Your eyes stare into mine with such longing
I surrender transfixed
Your lips open invite my tongue to enter
The pain! The excruciating pain!
You smile then turn and walk away
'I have never known such tenderness' you say.

You are ruthless in your generosity O goddess:
There is no thought which is not true
And beyond that - an ocean of meaning
Silver light glistens on its surface
Forms a mirror reflecting a clear sky
You put your finger to your lips and smile
'We are our own enemy everything is one'
There is either total acceptance or division
The frivolity of this and that
One potato two potato three potato four
It is simple far too simple to understand
So the clown cavorts the jester cries
As from a sullen darkness emerge the lies.

We look at the painting
What do you see?
What do I see?
Are these things to interchange?
If I could see through your eyes
And you through mine
Would we both see what is there?
Is anything there like what we see?
How can I know?
Yet you are quite certain
Doubt doesn't arise for you
Immersed as you are in the transient
What you see is true
The morning mist disperses
The harrowing world emerges hazy
And once again the sun circles
Your stationary glare
And I find myself dissolving
Like mist like salt pervading water.
You should be happy today
You have never been more right
It is just that for once
You would have preferred to be wrong
But you couldn't say that
And although you try and conceal
The pain that being right means
Something in your voice
In the way you look at me
A fleeting shadow
Speaks more than anything else
After all - words have such a hollow ring.

Swift swallow martins have all gone
The skies are clear and darkening
Small flocks of goldfinch in the field
Have found autumn food on cut grass
Hay is stacked maize awaits cutting
Leaves turning the hedgerow fruit is ripe
And after the frenzy of harvest – dying.

O goddess of deception Aphrodite
Weaver of illusions
Underneath your beauty is cunning
And the skill to trap your prey
You render me helpless
Before I am forlorn
Your charm destroys any hope
I may have had in my naivety
A simple truth conceals all
To turn away withdraw deny
Tortoise-like into fantasy
Enough to close your eyes
And it will vanish
What you do not wish to see
Death will not harm you
These children's tales tell
Of many happy rebirths
Being passed - a smiling bundle
From mother to mother
And your ears firmly shut
To what you do not wish to hear
But your realisation
Will be too late
And of what you do not
Want to know...Till then
Conceal your pain in a smile
And protect yourself
Until you no longer have control
Your friend does not love you
Those who do you ignore....

You resolve to change
Renew and rearrange
Every day a new sun shines
Every day a new life dies.

I see your face dissolve
As pleasure consumes
Like ice melting into air
Your smile smudges
As you wipe your mouth
Your eyes penetrate
Like fog in a hollow
And if I could offer anything
I know you would scorn it
'One day you will grow up
And will now look small'
As if you were ever tall!
Your words dribble down your chin
Not enough to cool your ardour
But I am immune to that now
I have turned into space
As eternal as I shall get
But my memory will remain
In the crevices of tomorrow
Where detritus too has new growth

Nocturnes

A flame arises before my eyes
Vermillion and gold
Tinged with cobalt and cerise
I watch it dance sinuously
Light becoming intense heat
And a tear of pain melts
Carving its groove on my cheek
Through a landscape
More primordial than that Night
When I wished I could hold you
Dancing before my eyes
O goddess - naked seductress
Always present.....always apart

The rain is hurled down
Like projectiles such force
A sudden storm wind
Tears the bushes seek
To uproot sweep them away
I watch still unmoving
A moment caught
Outside time perhaps grey
And then the sun again
As if nothing had changed
And you smile coyly
At the pool by the door
Where I stood watching
Your smile become a frown

I watch the evening light fade
And the silence descend
Permeated by darkness
A candle flickers
In the slight movement of breeze
Like the movement
Of your breath timid and intense
Then the sky is illuminated
Suddenly sliced through
My mind reels with the shock
I thought you were much closer
Until the scene recomposed
Leaving only memories
And traces of perfume
Scattered like blood on the ground
The scent of your prey waiting

I remember you in the evening
Wild geese flying across calling
Disturbing the sky before
Again falling silent
You had nothing to say
But looked beguiling
Your hair black as despair
And I struggled to resist
The fatal call I could hear
In the recesses of my mind
Slowly manifesting itself
In the slight tremour of my lips
And quiver of my dying thoughts

The rain washed against the window
Dark outside light shone in an arc
Revealing cropped grass in ghastly lustre
Your face in the room's shadows
Like a moon half-veiled by clouds
In the distance the call of a barn owl
Pierced like the cold steel of your stare
Even stones have more to share
You looked away gliding silently past
Eliding like a syllable with the Night

The mist swirls
In the early evening
With a flourish
And then quiescence
Alternating movement
As the wind gathers
And slackens
To suit the mood
Of the moment
Pianissimo sforzando
The vapour obscures
What might have been
Decisive clear
With the clarity
Of a bell that sounds
With the roundness
Of three dimensions
Dissolving again
To indistinctness
With the merest hint
Of forgiveness
Almost emerging
But like a wary
Small creature
Afraid of too much
Articulation
Withdrawing into
Open space
And waiting still waiting
For something to happen
Or the moment to subside
Resolved into the Night
And benediction of morning

The tenderness of moments
Near-forgotten recalled
At twilight between worlds
Ephemeral yet always hinting
At more much more
Than they can offer
Fingers touching lightly
On an arm or cheek
Like gossamer yet leaving
A sharp pain so refined
Its exquisite flowers
Blossom in a darkness
Concealing what it knows

Your kiss is sweet
It draws blood
Yours eyes mesmerise
In the distance
I hear the silence
Of a heron
Moving in to kill
Water pierced
My composure destroyed
As if I knew
What was coming, again

It's not the forgetting
It's the lies
The whole past rewritten
Person or people
Everything must align
With the new ideas
Lives are desecrated
The dead enslaved
No longer recognizable
To themselves
'I am someone else' -
Your silent marionette
Distorting hall of mirrors
This is how it is
Beginning with self-deception
Ending with a truth
More convenient than real

The Piety of History

The distinction between the historian and the poet is not in the one writing prose and the other verse - you might put the work of Herodotus into verse, and it would still be a species of history, it consists really in this, that the one describes the thing that has been, and the other a kind of thing that might be. Hence poetry is something more philosophic and of graver import than history, since its statements are of the nature rather of universals, whereas those of history are singulars.

('The Complete Works of Aristotle, Poetics', p. 2323, Vol 2. ed. Jonathan Barnes)

Hypatia

In death you became what others wanted
While you yourself were lost
Forensic scientists dissect your remains
To construct their fantasy woman:
Intelligent beautiful and politically adept
But you are still hidden concealed
In a light too brilliant to be seen
And such students! such forebears!
Your public face esteemed was apart
And few really knew the secrets you kept
In the end your very existence proved too much
The mob tore you apart in their sacred shrine
A heathen sacrificed to a greater god
Whose smile belied her flayed body
Less in your legend than in your life
Still you enchant, Hypatia
You who escaped who slipped away
In the commotion and piety of history

The silhouette of trees is spread around
The field's edge at the hedgerow
Sentinels in the evening
In the morning scanning the horizon
The hills fade submerge reappear
The distance moves closer is quite near
Then far away again
A pallid sun burns off October mist
A slow-burn intense light pervades
Then slowly blue then clear
Nothing remains the same
Not even the Night spreading like a stain
Immersing us in longing - though not for long
A new dawn brings new song
And the surprise of being alive
The silence pervades like space
Out of which all appears then disappears again
As my ears close then my eyes who knows?
Wait until the song stops
Until the silence
Between the sounds
Becomes all-pervasive
And in that space
Draw your future
Use bright colours
From a child's nursery
And always remember
For there is nothing else
That can help you identify
Your self or anything else
Your artistry imprinted
On an unknowable
Unutterable ground

Is a legacy that others
Will only take for granted
Not even the blinking of an eye
Or the curl of a lip
No acknowledgement
That anything at all
Is out of the ordinary
Extraordinary though it is
There is nothing further to say
Or sing.....

The mist swirls like a trumpet
Tentatively searching for a melody
So our talk sounded inebriated
Lacking any thread or coherence
Until I look around and you are gone

I open my eyes and begin to dream
I hear a piano in the room next door
Meandering impressionistically
The streets below are deserted
In my bed only your perfume remain

The thunder stopped only distant lightning
Remained its sudden nervous energy
Creating a spasm in the darkening sky
The shock a discharge of past memories
Stark warning an intimation calling
Across aeons to what might still happen
Always present in sly potentiality
Shadows are absorbed into the Night
Sounds into silence colours into pure light
The morning will be clear and fresh
Another dream opening unfathomably
Before your eyes dawning into a new day

Cave entrance into the Earth
Return to the enveloping womb
I shall sleep curled in foetal position
Unmoving and unmoved
Until I am possessed by a passing god
Or to you a passing fancy
Yet my words to those who hear them breathing
Will remain something different
Liberation upon hearing
While to you a mere beach littered
With starfish and the air filled
With the stench of the sea and decay

Leaves that have flown fall
Become mulch are absorbed
Into the Earth nourish new growth
Your words caught in mid-flight
Form on the page are preserved
They too can nourish new growth
In a cycle of life and death
Death and life chaos and form
The sun sets behind the hill
Swallowed into the sea
Like a surprise each morning
To reappear behind clouds
And mist or exposed to glare
The gaze of wasted lives
Awaiting a new harvest
In the sea of your sorrow
A new pain not yet experienced
Or an old wound erupting
In laughter again as you wait
Once more for the sun to set
Sinking behind a distant hill
Swallowed into a hollowing sea

They could find no evidence
He'd ever been alive
His face was blank
His hands turned to stone
There were no traces
Of a history - of encounters
With other people or things
Everyone claimed not to know
Anything about him
Something otherwise unknown:
Because a man's knowledge
Is much larger than his head
Not knowing is the best claim
To know - just like a smile
That means - 'Don't trust me
Like him - I'm fucked!'

You offer me flowers: cornflowers
Crimson roses fragrant white jasmine
Your silk chemise shimmers
Like light on rippling water
My closed eyelids form a screen
Receiving images my mind projects
And if I should open my eyes
Only a clear turquoise sky
With a golden sun the size of my thumb
And a mother-of-pearl moon appears
As through a glass blurred by tears

The ground is like a quagmire
The birds silent
Nothing else is moving
Total stillness
Until I see a hand turning
Slowly as if attached
To a dying body
Some errant god or goddess
Because even they are mortal
Fingers relaxing letting go
Such a relief no more pretence
They say there are words that escape
Slip through Indra's net
How could I know about that?
Morning begins slowly
Rising from darkness and rest
Into distraction where everything
Is regimented and good sense prevails
A well-ordered life
On which the sun never sets
Until the eyes grow heavy and dim
Now frailty prevails
And what was near becomes distant
Like lovers parting
Not even intense pleasure makes permanent
What was born to be no more than a part

Eight Songs for Zither and Accordion

Life's immeasurable bloom fell off in dark words like dust and breeze -

Novalis

1
Two goldfinches in Japanese maple
Susurration of leaves
Nothing moves

2
September: house-martins have flocked and fled
The dank night sky draws in
Stars pinpricks of light that point beyond
Though nothing is there
In silence the object's presence emerges
The radiance of things their fullness of being
An effulgence that offers more than it seems

3
Dank air…deflated moon
Torn and discoloured
What would you hope for?
Grain swells the harvest is ready
It is not your doing though you tried
It is beyond you…be thankful
To no one and nothing in particular
The sun fades over the horizon
Trailing behind it the dusk and dark…

4
Hedgerows burst with ripened blackberries
Red turned to black in autumn sun
Their sweet succulence dissolves in rapture
I open once again and again and melt within

5

Pierrot why so pale who tricked you?
You wring your hands look desolate
While behind your back they snigger
And would mock you if mocking hurt
You are past that there are no more tears
You are an empty husk the melancholy wind
Will whistle through though not revive
Your smile is now a grimace your benediction
The hollow hope of everlasting life

6

Ennui: the satin darkness
Illuminated from within
Black sun whose rite you enact
Fragment of a golden skin
Now prostrate voice of strangled praise
You strip anguished flesh from bone
Separate sinews from blood
In the darkness you atone
Their backs are turned indifferent
No pain can touch you now
Their blank faces smile grimace
Snigger outside the window
Shapes are hazy the stench
Of blood is heavy, eyes wide
Cannot reveal what is there
Coalescing in the void outside

7

Nobody came the door was open
Once there would have been
A visitor who would remain silent

Standing with an aura of sanctity
Or a naked woman seeking to entice
Now through the open door you see darkness
Merging with the darkness within
In the blinking of an eye
The edifice of your life crumbles
'Then ashes I was, not yet was I born'
You heard these words float in the air
A smoke curled upwards
Merged into the darkening space: Night
Rain fell the harvest is bountiful
And you were nowhere… were no one
How very much like living in another time
Another place…so very much the same

8
You tell him he is wrong, again
That you know
That the only evidence is yours
Words turn to water
Mix with salt tears, again
His mouth is dry his eyes
The bloom of flowers, hands of stone
And you know: looks cannot kill
Only adore… O yes, you know

As Mist Dissipates Into Sunshine

Perhaps the absolutely ineffable is ineffable in the sense that one cannot even state of it that it is ineffable.

(Damascius, 'De principiis', 1.10.22-4 tr. Opsomer)

1

Leaving Sylt by train we crossed the mudflat
causeway, artery to an island kept alive
as summer playground for rich politicians
media personalities, magnates.
Though from this place, and frequent visitor,
it's only now you make this pilgrimage
to the Nolde Stiftung Seebull. We arrive
in style by bicycle, hired at Neibull
where we disembarked; helped by following wind
that swirled among the crops, creating patterns,
large gestures from a painter's brush. We entered
to this other world, overcast, turbulent
where the artist retreated when he was banned
from painting, to create thirteen hundred
'Unpainted Pictures' in what became his tomb.
A quiet defiance in the name of Art and Life.

2

in excelsis deo

The hunt: the Master with a host
of lithe women in jodhpurs
bearing riding crops
O to be a blade of grass in their path,
or a pair of naked buttocks
offered to heaven

3

for James Low

And who am I? This bundle of memories,
sensations, perceptions
informed by ancient fictions
that only live in this imagined space
and are projected
onto the blank canvas of a landscape.
I exist in a dream I create that engulfs me,
from which I cannot separate -
it is one dream or another.
A dream that is shared,
arising though our common creations
then internalised -
(what is within comes from without)
that I then lay claim to - its mine, Me!
A kaleidoscope that configures,
each time slightly differently,
or with major disruption, severed, apart.

4

You call upon your past
to justify your actions now,
deny your agency you are
acting out a blueprint
implanted in you by others,
none of it is your doing,
neither that nor this, yet still
complain you feel trapped,
trapped and helpless -
why should you even try?
It is futile, pointless, nothing
will be different, you see yourself
caught in a web of others' making,
you retreat into self-pity:
no one could be more
self-preoccupied than you,
so self-absorbed, so sad,
through no fault of your own.
And there are always so many,
so many more to blame,
Not-me is always the sole focus
of your attention; it must be
really tiring with all that burden
dragging everywhere, and longing
for a solitude you will not fit,
that cannot hold you. Nothing,
no one can hold you while you remain
fixated by your doom,
and the inadequacy of your legacy
that makes you only what you are.

5

'Water Serpents' on Kublick's Mahler was my
first encounter with Klimt, bought on a whim.
I'd never heard of Mahler, then suddenly
a new world opened, patchwork of human
moods and feelings. At the Palazzo Strozzi
in Florence, surprised, I stumbled upon
this decadent again: an exhibition
of Klimt's paintings, remnants of the Belle
Epoque. Then ten years later in Liverpool
with others, mother and daughter, in secession,
very fin de siècle. Poor Vienna
had its heart torn out, and thoughts of war to cleanse
and purify the individual and the race,
like spores carried on the wind, flourished.
Now I too felt trapped, knowing some doom approached
yet in denial, and incredulous.

6

for Martin Boord

The crystalline light of an early January afternoon
ice needles of pain bring tears to my eyes
where there was once joy, flickering, fleeting
like silvery fish emptied from captive nets
flashing their brilliance as they expire,
transformed, inert, to become mere nourishment
to titivate the vacant palate of some bored bystander
whose life is consumed by want.
Here, I stand with all this space around me:
fields hedges woods and a steely wind
that stabs and slashes dry contracted flesh;
alone again, but this time open
like a yogi in an Himalayan cave, not stranded
in the midst of an alien people
whose language seems to be my own, but isn't;
or perhaps I only imagine that I speak.
Tears harrow my cheeks like chiselled stone.
Unmoving, I could have grown here
over centuries, or been reclaimed; but no one else
is around, only the sun's light through the clouds.

7

for Keith Dowman

He stepped out of the jungle onto, as it were, a stage set,
and under a banyan tree near to fragile dwellings
sat cross-legged like a lotus risen out of the mud,
perfectly still he attracted attention;
it was unusual for someone to settle like that here
like a heron watching, waiting - the invisible
made visible - while the people congregated.
He wore an flayed human skin over one shoulder,
his hair long and matted was tied up in a top-knot,
unkempt, unwashed, his body smeared with ashes
from the corpses he lived among in the charnel ground
where he shacked-up with his pox-ridden mistress, a slut, a
chavette.
This layabout, university drop-out, depraved and degraded
social outcaste, whose presence mocked the righteous
and holy clerisy, intellectuals, hard-working families;
someone who to the bourgeoise stank like curdled milk,
an affront to all that was held sacred and revered.
He played his damaru and sang with a voice
rough and unmelodious, yet captivating;
the words seemed simple yet were incomprehensible
as he rasped and grated to a hypnotic rhythm
that astonished and distracted from the everyday banality.
And then - he ended abruptly and it was silent,
he withdrew into the jungle again as if he had
never been there - his presence an illusion.
Yet like half-remembered dreams,
or wisps of smoke from last night's fire,
traces of song, strange and haunting remained,

reverberating in the brain and tissues of the body.
And a young man, recognising that everything is of one taste
without glancing back, followed his footsteps into the jungle
divesting himself… leaving a trail of clothes,
becoming one with the trees with the wind with the world,
as he disappeared like clouds, leaving a clear blue sky.

8

for Chris Coppock

The undead, how we await them
to arise and open their eyes,
mere shadows in a fractured sun;
they behave as if they were alive,
appear indistinguishable to the living.
But rocks turn to scree, scree to sand
this high up - closer to the gods
than the gods are to us - more inward.
But can we be proud of this?
Call them our achievements?
The ghosts we project and make real,
ourselves given forms we don't recognise,
and the music, shrill, shattering the silence
which falls like splinters
refusing to configure in any meaningful shape,
as anything familiar and comforting.
And when we look around at all that is familiar,
it is alien, like a song we thought we knew,
in another language, somewhere we have never been.

9
We have looked at objects
until our eyes have turned to stone
and awareness become dust
So, where is the grit? you say.
You don't have to look far:
it is under your torn fingernails

10
Someone shakes my shoulder - 'Are you awake?
Wake up! The sky is clear, the light radiant.'
In the room it is dark. I turn over, sleep on.
You too inhabit my dreams - like falling stars.

11

I read this elaboration of Shantarakshita
by Mipham, like a severe music trapped
in stone, light struggling to emerge. At times
exasperated, pre-emptory, a master dealing
with recalcitrant, inattentive pupils, his
impatience crashing like shattered glass,
shards glistening in the sun's rays, escaping
the oppression of clouds and a sudden hail.
This is the ladder you ascend, the words
the reasons rigorous and sharp, until you reach
the open window and enter in to clear
unelaborated space, pure luminosity.
Yet everything remains the same, nothing
appears, made manifest: this spoon, this cup
present just as they appear to be
yet something more. What, I could not say.

12

In vain I look for fieldfare, redwing.
Once in small flocks in late autumn
and snipe from frozen moorland
by our stream seeking refuge, then
as mists descended and icy winds
from the north brought early snow
the sun white in a pallid sky, silent:
so many secrets… and nothing said.

13

Two ravens in silhouette
on the branch of a bare tree
The sky a silvery grey.
There's a light breeze
otherwise it is still, until
a third appears, and all three
fly to the ground, eat millet
before flying away
leaving dark shadows
in the light of a fading mind.

14

Magnolias in bloom, airborne lotus;
pale in the dusk, as colour fades.
Devoid of light, so much lost. Recollections
still in shadows. Maybe never to emerge, open.

15

I see your face, your skin glows
like light reflected off a black sun,
smooth like a becalmed sea;
whether there is a depth beyond that
I do not know - it is beyond all knowing

16

for Jeanne Openshaw

Less medieval, more a country house hotel
with tourist attractions attached, zen garden
discretely placed not to obtrude, or just
an outdoor cinema or theatre,
whatever will entertain, distract and earn.
Yet Tagore was here in body and in
inspiration, a small Shantineketan
at Dartngton, where once unknown to me
my future teacher lived who you,
my fellow Sanskrit student, must have met there.
Strange how thing can connect and patterns weave
a tapestry without loose ends. Still, some
can lose their way: devotion is not strong
enough, the application lacking, are left
to seek a vision where only stones abound.

17

I think of your cold cruelty,
the beauty, as you manipulate
and manoeuvre to maintain
the moral high ground.
Outside leaves wither and fall.
The air is chill, sun a mockery,
and I contract into a black hole
from which no light can escape,
and another world is destroyed.

18

You will not benefit from my death, she said.
He offered his life like a still warm egg,
so she could be with her only child again;
and it would have slipped gently from her hands
had he not pre-empted, and rudely smashed it.

19

Laugh! I laughed so much
my face dissolved
in the acid of my tears
… O exquisite perfume

20

To be free - to have my wants
fulfilled, though insatiable, and really
for something else. To be controlled by forces
I do not know and barely recognise:
This is freedom. Let me shout it from the
rooftop before I jump. And then one Spring
confounded by those greens I cannot paint
I retire into the coven of your charms,
and never ask if the absurd and noble
Spinoza is right - such a burden borne
in isolation, ostracised, denying
the presence of your arms, and captivated
by desires I never knew I had till now.
Withdrawn into imagination there's
nothing there that is not real, the world a dream
I struggle to wake from before I die.

21

The Jokhang is a mere museum now
all sense of geomancy gone;
drained of vitality the silent forms
do not reach out or speak,
enveloped in their own stillness
they dare not move.
The guards are watchful,
the visitors groping in the dark.
Outside the sky is clear, translucent, blue.
What can I see that is not there?
No Chinese princess now,
Only a soldier with his boots and gun
And new antiquities deprived of sense.
This darkness like a cave conceals,
in plain view, the secret that you seek
more vividly than in daylight,
if you adjust those eyes you thought could see:
Yes, I am less than everything you thought of me.

22

for Paul Messam

Early January in Aswan, the night was black,
the air still warm. Along the corniche Nile cruisers
were mored; across the water Kitchener Island's
botanic gardens lay engulfed by shadows,
We found somewhere to eat, a local cafe
far from tourist haunts, and returned
to the Cataract Hotel through the deserted souk;
nearby still stood the Coptic church of St George,
where people spilled onto the pavement
like a football crowd when the game is up:
its lights so bright, the building so large and brash.
I met Pope Shenouda in Stockport once,
with my wife, a Copt, and was impressed by his
austere presence. Afternoons we took tea
on the hotel terrace overlooking the feluccas
on the Nile, as the sun set. Last time I was here
I caught a train to Cairo overnight, an old French train,
arriving next morning to a family reunion.
There is nothing like Cairo.
How many families have I had? Lived in how many houses
not mine? Who chooses how their life will go
once the comfort of a living death's eschewed?
Where will you find yourself? When will you stop looking,
when all that phantasmagoria starts to fade with age?

The Radiance Of Light

If the towering white clouds mount into the broad heavens.
If the bleak days scare away all shining radiance, and if all breadth
shrivels into the paltriness of narrow conventionality, then the heart
must remain the source of what is light and spacious.

('Ponderings' V.7, p.231, Martin Heidegger, trans. R. Rojcewicz)

…beneath matter, beneath experience, beneath words, something that
is different from them..

('In Search of Lost Time' Vol. VI, Time Regained, p.254, Marcel
Proust, trans. Moncrieff & Kilmartin)

Naturally Occurring Mandala

for David Noyce

1.
Resplendent in silken white, the royal bridegroom,
Skin translucent like the inner nacre of abalone,
With gentle smile, tranquil, and in perfect repose.
Others become calm in your presence, the storm ceases,
Turbulence subsides, to return to that open-expanse
Of your endless arms, illuminated from within.
Nothing is solid enough to exclude or divide -
No fractions or factions, just like the silence that
Pervades all words, all syllables, all space. Still….

2.
The rock stands erect, alone, adamantine,
Like a code that will not crack
To reveal its secrets; a solitary finger
Defiant, sticking out of the sea where swell
And froth churns around its base.
Disturbed by pride, a paranoia
Fraught with isolation, when calmer
Seas reveal things as they are: a mirror
To a cloudless sky, vast, immobile, clear.

3.
Earth's riches: azure skies, the barley
Glistens in the field like gold.
It is autumn - the days are drawing-in.
Soon a jewel-like frost will cover
The hardened ground, no longer yielding,
And then restored will give again

With boundless generosity. Like fecund mother
You look on all with equanimity,
None more favoured, each a precious gem.

4.
Before me you sit, serene and radiant, like a ruby.
In the West, the sky is red with gold and violet,
As the sun dips down behind the horizon.
Here, it is still, peaceful; the wind has calmed
And in the sharp light I can distinguish each thing
Before it dissolves, with others, into darkness.
Within there is limitless light, now subdued
(Nothing is without shadow where there is light)
In which dreams manifest as vivid as any day.

5.
It is the green of summer, grass blowing
In the wind, creating a pattern, a dance,
Caressing the naked skin and sending
A frisson through her body, creating
A future with an apparently random wave
Of the hand in a display of fearlessness,
Even if not fully comprehended. Jealous?
I don't think so, but somehow forceful,
Forceful like a strong, fierce wind from the North.

Eyes close on a vacuity within,
yet voices ricochet from dream
to tenuous dream; only fragments
are caught, like shards, unearthed
by gloved hands, that don't cohere.
As if, somehow, it all made sense
once. Now, all that remains
evaporates under an aberrant sun;
tears trickle down an uncomprehending
face that is slowly, slowly, turning into stone.
Translucent blue where sky and sea meet
are one at the horizon that absorbs the sun:
an eye that closes to reveal a satin darkness
caressing trees, houses, the endless sands;
tempting silence with a stealth that seethes,
while dreams emerge like pink crustaceans,
timid creatures that can't stand the scrutiny of day
creating fears you never knew you had, hope
drained away till dawn renews with gentle rain and light.
Nothing will last, what you clutch will break,
so hold it lightly, keep it fresh and moist…
Too old to mourn now, eyes too dry…
It changes nothing, nothing changes in its course.
Appearances deceive and you deceive yourself;
a hand once soft and small turns into bark
that no one wants to hold unless in pity, you see
reflected in their eyes, as in an empty sky that clouds,
Occluding thoughts, that quietly panic, are distraught.

Sunset over the North Sea.
Sky streaked violet, gold, red,
a dying imperium we watch
from an island barely afloat.
A constant battle to sustain,
time runs through your fingers,
and each tear you don't cry
chokes your ability to lie:
There is no turning away -
only the sound of a hungry sea
ravenous to consume the land
You stretch out on lithely, and pray.

Diptych

One

1

'Her Majesty's Servant', pious pursuer of papists,
Richard Topcliffe, psychopath, rack master
And ransacker, of serpentine handwriting
And lewd imagination: fantasising out loud
Of groping Her Majesty's nipples, tits, and soft belly
Under her skirt, while stretching an innocent victim
Who, not recanting, was made to stand two hours
On the gallows' ladder, in shirt alone, before swinging.
Her Majesty, sponsor of terror, fedei defensatrix
Of the Protestant God, whose love is unquenchable,
Always mindful in her righteousness of the Last Judgement.

2

Even by God called 'god', fraternal regicide
Murderer, torturer, by proxy of course,
Whose bounteous compassion stopped short
Of alleviating the suffering of her people
Whose goods she held in trust. 'God save my people'
She proclaimed in passing, post-menopausal Gloriana,
Hoping to elicit a fabulous response: 'We adore you'.
Good Queen Bess, portrayed by that traitor to truth
The faithful William Camden in his 'Annales'.
Unquestioned for centuries, author of her ethereal sepulchre.
Requiescat in pace, indeed, let truth slumber, embalmed.

3

Consider Southwell, sweet Robert, whose submission
Was taken as treason, who only the execution crowd
Had compassion for, sparing him the Queen's diktat:
That he be cut down from the gallows the moment
The ladder was kicked away, one swing of the rope,
And before stopping breathing be disembowelled
Fully conscious, flesh and bone hacked back
Beyond the ribs so he could watch heart and entrails
Burning as he expired - O gentle Queen.
His response: 'May she enjoy all gifts of nature
And grace, all help of friends and faithful councillors',
Rejoicing in God's glory may she inherit the Kingdom.
'Have mercy on him', the crowd replied, 'have mercy'.

4

Christian champion, whose beautiful pallor
Was as toxic as her acts; washed in egg white,
Powdered egg shells, alum, borax, camphor oil,
Lemon juice, white poppy seed and plant extract
Dissolved in a health-giving spring water,
Skin treated with ceruse, vinegar, turpentine
And quick silver, enrouged with cochineal or vermillion.
But nothing could disguise the ugliness within
Not even her Jewish physician, abandoned to death,
Could treat that wracked body or mind, so full of disease.
Her smile, yellow and black, concealed behind
A perfumed silk handkerchief; hairless,
She shrouded her intent in deceit.
Today, what would the newspapers say?

The truth more deeply concealed and contorted,
The agony of a dying age that can't let go:
Gloria, gloria in excelsis deo. Angels we have heard on high.

Two

Emperor Ashoka's Song:
May all beings live in peace
And in harmony together,
May diverse religions flourish
Like plants in a variegated border;
Free from the slaughter
And silent denial of monoglots -
The righteous convinced
Of their own way and intolerant
Of dissent, exclusive in their claims.
May all beings have open hearts
Towards others, whoever they are,
Wherever they come from or reside;
Embrace all without exception
Recognising human frailties
And the ignorance of confusion,
May they be protected from harm
By those out of control or blinded
By the lust for domination,
And those who desecrate the truth
To achieve their selfish, misguided, ends.

May people be free and tolerant
Accepting and celebrating
Differences as well as similarities,

May animals and their habitats
Be protected and treated kindly;
The Earth, of which we are part,
Be nourished and not exploited.
Whatever small good I may have done
I dedicate to the well-being others
And take upon myself
The negative results of their actions.
Through the cultivation
Of wholesome states of mind,
And elimination of unwholesome ones,
May all beings everywhere
Know peace and happiness,
And goodwill towards others flourish.

Transitions

Unoriginate,
pure presence,
in which all emerges;
phenomena manifest.

We see
your absence,
in the presence of a tree,
silhouetted
against evening sunset.

Like a cut-out
from the landscape
revealing,
infinite darkness,
at the foot of which
tears well.

It is silent,
the wind is still.

Soon all
is to be enclosed
in the plangent
melancholy of night.

The music
shimmers and fades.
A solitary moon
remains
like a thumb-
print the sky
cannot erase.

Like a magical apparition
destined to vanish,
your failure
to understand my nature,
your judgements
of whatever you call
whatever manifests;
the resultant
desire and attachment,
create
a substantive vision
you believe in falsely.
And you wander -
a blind man
tapping his cane,
creating
a profligate story
that soothes,
and quietly dismays.

Circumambulating the hall of liberation,
it didn't rise. O Allen,
where are you? Your howl is lost
across generations;
your pain sanitised, analysed, become
a text: lost in the whiteness of the page.
Liberated from what? Changing one oppression
for another - another story;
another half-known, reconstructed inspiration
and a second beginning?
Thirty-six heroic figures - the new pantheon;
with eighteen goddesses in attendance.
No stupa, no liberation for the heavy mind,
obscured, burdened with cares,
lost in a maze of thoughts:
a secular mandala that will not transcend
mundane preoccupation.
Praises rise upwards, caught in stone,
darkness remains within, alone.
 Listening to 'Freddie Freeloader' in Passau,
sitting in Anton's cafe with macchiato:
the square is deserted, almost;
St Stephens squats, a huge toad transfigured
that once intoned ethereal angelic orisons,
while inside, an infernal organ in the cathedral bowels,
presentiment of hell, execrates the grandeur of a Name.
So far away - a pulse at the outer universe's edge
undetectable by sense - Hope, a flicker on a screen.
Yet now, Miles, no miles, just seven steps to heaven,
no cherub in sight, and presence more divine than lost.

Valhalla, yet a Greek temple
perched on a limestone hilltop
rising above a forest over the Ister -
a renewal of ancient rights?
This culture too will soar again,
pallid and well-proportioned,
a sign that despite all, its spirit
has long expired and won't revive
through strength of will, or aspiration.
Destroyed on the pyre of Rome.
This dream in stone too ethereal
to be more than a ghastly presence
haunting the minds of those for whom,
alone, dissatisfaction or despair remains.

No point knocking at an empty house
where only the past could answer.
The gods have fled, and people
stand blankly around, then fixate,
doing anything they can. They voyage
into forgetfulness, busy, distracted.
Hart Crane remembered much…
….no longer recognised.
Despite feeling something's missing,
there is so much happening.
A meteor-shower
that informs as transiting through space
between stars, between planets
between two deaf ears
and articulates as knowledge:
'This I know…..I am…'.
How cruel deceit reshapes a world
It takes as new. Here in the doorway
I stand and wait for…I know not what now,
Devoid of hope, only like a tree that weeps.
Sailing into Vienna, the suburbs
much the same as anywhere;
the Ister pauses and we disembark.
The sky clear and blue.
The water brown and trembling.
We see the contrast, old and new
on different banks. Each celebrates
in its own way: imperious and ordered,
assertive and arrogant; two ages
embrace in their rupture, facing
a past and future that doesn't fit.
A cold hand embraces stone.
We speak but do not understand.

Words fall like stars
into the abyss of incoherence.
Only night brings all together in her
indiscriminate and indeterminate smile.

Predicates of Being

Words rise like birds
startled, wheeling round:
diamond-like eyes.
Only what is abandoned
is understood.
It is not a lot to carry
secreted on your person.

There was snow, the shards of crystals
containing a rainbow.
A boot, tattered and worn
with the dust of aeons
covering, dragged
though many lives and places I do not know.
Today, only a threadbare dream
and haunting music that fades
as soon as it touches the ground -
heart melting in the warmth of your pain.

There are the spaces
between objects,
between hills,
where Nothing manifests;
between sounds,
translucent silence:
The elegance of presence.

The shape of sadness, Amadeo
drawn-out note of tears,
and the texture of ruffled velvet,
(It is hot in here,
I feel I too am melting,
melting under your gaze).
An elongated hand.
It could be an icon,
window onto eternity,
within which my silent prayer
(Is mist on a glass dissolving….

The birds
fall
like leaves
in Autumn
and
rise again.
Above
the sun circles
obscured
by clouds:
so many sparrows.

Nothing to see - keep looking;
your hand strikes ice,
an incandescent sunset
blazes across the tundra.
Do you think
there is anything else to say,
or is *that* the problem?
Who knows… how you do it….

Like a space-traveller:
sky filled with rainbow light,
leaving nothing.
Elements dissolve,
and I had no idea:
no preference.
Modest as an empty plate,
no reference point,
and without the slightest suggestion

In no time at all,
watching, waiting,
a sparrow alights;
hedgerow already alive
what is one more?
What are you seeing -
one or more?
There are no more…
A group of Khamper traders
at the market at Shigatse
laughed and howled
pointing in my direction.
We approached to inquire
what was so funny:
'albino', they said, 'like us
only white'. Which sums it up:
Appearances - only skin deep.

I am a child of the sixties, you of the seventies.
This year you are sixty, next I am seventy.
That's one hundred and thirty years between us,
enough you might think for some wisdom to arise,
but sadly, wisdom doesn't come with age but with folly.
Staying within the rules may be clever, but is it wise?
It is not knowing rather than knowing; knowing
is the turgid embrace of death, a rigour mortis
that encases life, unlike the softness, the fallibility of a child:
If you catch that thought arising, or that tone
when you speak, fill your ears with strawberries
and skip all the way to the sea, watching as it slowly recedes.

Wynter Fall

I discern forms emerging
as from a fog,
give them a name and measure.
We greet and then they pass
like ghosts. I too dissolve,
to reappear elsewhere, as someone else.
The name you call me floating
away like gossamer.
The footprint filled with water in the flood.

Only the hair and nails remain,
whatever else, is gone:
his body like a mist in sun.
The one you cling to is not there.
You dream, but when you close
your eyes, all present disappears.
Only darkness conceals
what you might have known,
and anything you might have been.
Silence absolves all sounds.
Finally, the name too dissolves -
as if there was never anybody there.

Darkness descends.
Yet cupped
in your hands a flame
still flickers.
Just close your hands.
The light extinguishes
and that is all, all that remains.

Your body is an implement
that shucks open
the world, to reveal
a void containing a pearl.
In its unobstructed space,
the wind stirs, blows
through the universe.
The flame fanned flares.
Earth emerges from the ocean,
Translucent palace
crowns an ancient mountain,
until you empty your hands,
and all vanishes - like sand.

'First, know yourself, and then relate'.
Ah! but you thought you knew.
Intoxicated on the lies you told,
failing to see how you arise,
your exploits laying others at your feet,
you assumed a false identity,
dressed the part, but those you suppress
are not you, and emerge
in a separateness you cannot accept.
It is only you who have forgotten
who you are, confounded in deceit,
you struggle to be something you are not.

Unable to accept things as they are
you pursue a dream into despair,
and once the spell is broken, no-one
owes you anything, only angry shades
taunt from the shadows, and isolation
is your prize, as you drum a broken shell.
Not recognising what has hatched -
yes, it is you! - and what is still unseen,
you can construct, if you remember how.
When all excuses, all alibis have gone
perhaps you will embrace a new humility,
recognise what you are, accept yourself
and what you have become, then share
a voice with others you can call your own.

In all those years we were never close,
and the distance between has only grown,
estranged by a divide that knows no name,
you didn't nurture or inspire,
and for each tear I shed you lied;

your grandeur just a camouflage -
elaborate concealment of a void
leaving nothing to embrace but space
and air that's so refined I cannot breathe,
not borne on such exalted heights as you.

Cold indifference you displayed
Haughty and remote, you still withdrew
further as your delusions flourished,
discarding to rapacious fate
what hope was ripe for exploitation.
And still, you say, 'Sing my praises,
I am the soil in which you grew.'
A soil devoid of nutrients for me,
waste ground, rubble-strewn, contaminated,
haunted by a yellow fog that suffocates.

'Forget my history, look at what I stand for,
my ideals' - and I have seen and felt
the power of your ideals, where my home was,
the ruthlessness and hate that is your history,
for which acceptance is beginning of recovery
not escape; for, if you cannot live with yourself
without repressing truth, how can others?

I am everywhere I perceive or imagine,
the house itself is empty and on fire;
inseparably other, we construct a tale,
a tale that changes or that ossifies,
a character that's clothed in flesh
through which it lives a life fantastical

in this common dream we share.
This tapestry, a replica, its threads
woven with care, devoid of anything that moves,
caught in a stasis only death endows
with melancholy music and vacant stares
as you slowly realise..no-one was ever there.
For those who have lost someone
for the alone, bereft, abandoned,
those without country or home,
the rejected, ejected, unprotected,
in the darkness of this shortest day
may we recognise the transience of clouds
and with life, the inevitability of light.

Spring snow arrives.
So many birds
Leaving no trace:
We form what forms us.

Sea spray, silver light
on water, sand compact
under foot, oyster-catcher
at water's edge, little gulls
watch as sea recedes,
surfers follow waves to ride,
and these figures walking
across the beach, firm as mist…

Nothing much separates us,
more an isthmus than a gulf,
yet still beyond reach,
despite hands that touch,
smiles that soften, distance.
Even when I hold you,
you are somewhere else
wondering where I am.
The only thing we converge in
is separation: I shall wade
into the estuary, while you forage
amidst the upland gorse.
In spite of everything we remain
close, only somewhere else.

Among hedgerows, outside the window
of the wooden cabin, birds flit:
blackbird, chaffinch, sparrow
and sweet-natured collared dove.
One pauses and looks into
the dark interior. What does she see?
Perhaps some sullen beast, contained
restrained in time, that seeks
obliteration of them, their home, of life;
pursuing an illusory dream, regurgitation
of fractured, unknit infancy. So, slowly
slowly the tides recede, without return
devoid of time, future, hope, crippled love.

It is dark. The air is heavy, pink
and gold. An evening rainbow
arches above the village near
the church; bells ringing across
the valley fields beneath,
ringing doom not joy and maybe,
just maybe it is better to die
oblivious still, in denial, or perhaps
one last 'Hurrah!' The last idea
passing with the last man, cradled,
tended by the last woman, alone.

Once more the evening's stealth conceals the change,
day slipping away unheralded into forgetfulness;
a life passing as so many more. If you could pile them
all like grains of sand, how vast the mountain range
overshadowing with its own distinctive climate,
and nothing unaffected, no one the cause, struggling on
to freely choose, until there is no plain, nor any action
of your own, and everything was hoped, was hoped
in vain, until in darkness we are blessed with sleep again.

The silence, tangible
like sculpted ice,
smile that's frozen,
body turned away,
your voice is simply -
lips that move, yet
more you couldn't say.
No explanation,
no elaboration,
nothing intellect could
mechanically engage;
a solitary presence
in all its eloquence
reveals all there is
to know, if only someone
else was there also.

Our eyes meet, and behind the shutters the pain;
compacted, forged into an artefact
that adorns a presence still not fully there.
You whisper, in a voice seeking to withdraw;
a tongue's lick, seeping into crevices,
leaving a dampness, knowing it has been touched.
Who, what, has been touched? Yours eyes obscured
by clouds, tears fall hard as gunshot
and I am confused. Don't know where to turn.
I feel the pellets penetrate, explode inside,
as we struggle to maintain a calm demeanour,
as if nothing is happening, nothing we can't overlook.
The day opens like an old scroll I can't decipher,
in a script I never learned, rent and stained with blood.
I reach out to touch you, but too late
everything has disappeared and again my eyes close.

The rowan, filled with sparrows,
heavy with berries.
Cacophony of calls orchestrating
days drawing in;
once height of summer, fully gone:
insanity breeds insanity.
Sane alone worried, at margins,
we forget. Little changes
just reconfigures, reforms, escapes.
Why struggle to remove this
Mount of Bodies, where scree tumbles
into shimmering lake below?
As we wait, mist descends; enables
us to forget anything we knew:
a mother's touch, her eyes, our presence.

The Philistines are here - as if they'd ever gone!
Hiding under stones, in crevices, among rocks?
O no - they reside in comfort and complacency,
in bourgeois settlements: some even paint
or write poetry; the veneer of course tarnished
now pretence and self-deception are over.
They screw-up courage, turn swarthy backs
on a rabid future of art, culture, enlightenment,
stinking of the dung they smeared on pallid bodies,
beatific smiles reflecting profound self-satisfaction,
a newly discovered nakedness the badge of pride.
'Rough-hewn' are words of praise, their anthem
a rhythmic chant of terraces enthralled to violence,
wilful provocation, high-spirited bores, national disease,
like love best served cold, and with indifference.

You want to carry
a burden of dogma?
Far better to have
a belly full of food.
You are crazy
with your ideas, iron
fist of determination,
holding together
the fragile tissue
of lies you were told,
betrayal you felt.
Not your fault,
but avidly consumed
in your desperation.
Not for you the play
of sunlight through words,
sparkle of tremulous water,
feel of baked ground underfoot.
No, you know, and are
transported beyond that,
inhabiting an invisible world
you struggle to bring
into existence, and doing so
obscure all your senses
could tell you;
and beyond that -
all the mirror could show.

'Only the sky remains', when eyes are closed, and all around
dissolves back into space, all ruinous testimony gone,
deceased as is the hubris that is man, the effort meaningless;
the struggle of blind will, once lauded, now forgotten:
there is nothing to remember, only scars healing over him
and *this* sky, this vast expanse of stillness and of peace.

The sky is darkening, rain begins.
Wind ruffles trees' hair.
In my cabin I feel the onslaught,
my mind darkens, as light drains.
This storm did not occur
with suddenness but spent years
configuring as charms expired,
leaving these unreclaimed tears.
It will soon be over, we just sit tight,
as each in the other's absence atones.

Rowan berries, ripe, weigh
branches down; young
blackbirds peck among
gravel and grass around;
storms after summer sun
shake trees and slake
their thirst, plants revive
and promise revenue.
As for the rest? Less foible,
grandeur of self-destruction,
driven by rage, confusion, greed.
How far can it stretch,
accommodate, bestow benign
regard before it snags and breaks?
There have been floods, and more:
the carnage of delusions;
as one more dream consumes,
draws quiet voices out, subdues.

Rootless Tree

www.elysianwiles.com